D0455384

essence of WOOD

Hilary Mandleberg

essence of WOOD

HarperResource
An Imprint of HarperCollins*Publishers*
www.harpercollins.com

Designer   Luis Peral-Aranda
Editor   Sophie Bevan
Location Research Manager   Kate Brunt
Production   Patricia Harrington
Art Director   Gabriella Le Grazie
Publishing Director   Alison Starling

First published in Great Britain in 2000
by Ryland Peters & Small

ESSENCE OF WOOD
Text copyright © Hilary Mandleberg 2000
Design and photographs copyright
© Ryland Peters & Small 2000

All rights reserved. No part of this publication
may be reproduced in whole or in part or
stored in a retrieval system, or transmitted
in any form or by any means, electronic,
mechanical, photocopying, recording, or
otherwise without written permission of the
publisher. For information regarding permission,
write to HarperCollins, 10 East 53rd Street,
New York, NY 10022.

Library of Congress Cataloging-in-Publication
Data available on request
ISBN 0-688-17433-7

10 9 8 7 6 5 4 3 2 1

Printed and bound in China by
Toppan Printing Co.

contents

fire & shelter

Fire and shelter are two of life's essentials. Wood generously offers both. It warms us and enables us to prepare our food. It protects us from wind and rain, sun, and snow.

For millions of years, wood has been a mainstay of human existence. It has provided us all with one of the most beautiful, versatile, and durable of our building materials, and in many parts of the world, it is still an important source of fuel. For a great number of

ELEMENTAL STRUGGLE

our ancestors, supplies of wood were readily available for building. It was a good insulator and protected from the elements. To make a wall, people could gouge notches in logs and just stack them one on top of the other. Or they could use slices of entire tree trunks

to construct a framework, filling the
gaps with a mixture of mud and twigs.
As techniques developed, they learned

to cut wood into boards or tiles. Laid
centuries ago in overlapping patterns,
they still keep homeowners dry today.

natural

In a rural setting, nothing beats wood that seems to have come straight from the forest. It breathes life into the building and gives us a spiritual link with nature and with ancient beliefs. In Norse mythology, Yggdrasil was a great ash tree that held heaven in its

THE SPIRIT WORLD

branches, the underworld in its roots, and all temporal life in its vast trunk. Bring this sense of wonder into your home with the hefty grandeur of giant logs, the unique twists and turns of bark-covered branches, the cracks and fissures that tell of a tree's history.

Rough-hewn logs bring a
pioneering spirit to a cool
contemporary interior.

Partnership with nature is essential for life. Follow the natural curves and rhythms of wood to show your respect.

contemporary

Wood can be adapted to any number of locations and to all historical periods. One of the motifs of the last hundred years has been man's domination of nature, so it is no surprise to find that in the modern home, our wood reflects this theme. We cut, plane,

NATURE TAMED

sand, and polish it into smooth, sleek shapes that emphasize its matchless grain and texture. We slice it into thin veneers and bend it into the most wondrous shapes. We combine it with chrome and leather and steel. In short, we force it to obey our rules.

Wood sets the scene in style. An inspirational chair brings new life to bentwood design. Sheets of perfectly matched veneer are the friendly face of organized living. Plywood-lined walls and stairs of solid ash are warm yet functional.

decorated

Decorated wood leads us into new realms of beauty where woodcarvers and turners, artists and decorators reign supreme. The urge to embellish our homes is a primitive one, and wood offers us many possibilities. We can order our walls and staircases

ALL DRESSED UP

paneled and stenciled, our bedposts carved, our stair rails turned to form spiraling twists, our floors laid in blocks or precision-edged with the finest inlay, our roofs fretted into hearts and flowers, and our knick-knacks graced with light-as-air motifs.

living spaces

The purpose of wood in nature is to provide the strengthening and water-conducting tissue in the stems and roots of trees and shrubs, but what versatility it offers us in the home! Wood's strength and weight vary from species to species, so different woods

TIMELESS & VERSATILE

suit different purposes. Softwoods are easy to cut; hardwoods have a closer grain and take a high polish. Their colors vary widely, too, from the white of holly, through the hues of giant redwoods to the black of ebony. Some woods have a natural luster or—as in

the case of cedar—an aroma from the essential oils they contain. The most beautiful woods are often sealed and polished to show off their good looks, while others are painted or stained to hide their origins. Wood suits classic or modern homes. Painted and molded paneling conjures up period elegance; unadorned woodwork evokes the honest values of Shaker life; the rugged grain of marine plywood or the cool tones of bare ash create oases of calm in the stress-filled world of today.

Wood will fit all your decorating needs.
Rich polished wood takes a traditional
room to new heights. Hefty oak planks

and graceful bentwood make a success
of dining. Exposed roof, walls, and
floor evoke a spacious medieval hall.

Do you wish to sleep
high under the eaves?
Whether you long for
pared-down pastels or
for cozy chintz quilts,
you must have wood.

Wood's rustic beauty takes shape in a bathroom lined with hefty logs. Dainty lamps and pastels give a lighter look.

accessories

From tiny toothpicks to fine furniture, there are an estimated ten thousand different products made of wood, and of these, home accessories are but a few. Wood brings us plates and bowls that warm the heart and finely turned flatware, cups, boxes, and frames that

BEAUTY & UTILITY

feel smoothly sensuous to the hand. It needs only a little imagination to transform a collection of twigs and branches into a lamp base straight from the woods, or to visualize a delicate shade made from the timeless art of steaming and bending veneer.

outside

Nowhere is wood more at home than outdoors. Trees are our planet's lungs and are now a focus of people's environmental concerns. As long as we take care of them, they will repay us by providing for our needs. Wood outdoors is a must for anyone who

AL FRESCO

loves nature. See how a wooden house rising tall in the midst of a glade or perched beside a forest-edged lake is wholly at one with its surroundings. And painted or plain, wooden porches and verandas are where indoors and outdoors meet. Take a seat and watch

the world go by from a rustic bench, or settle into deep, yielding cushions. Mark your space with a picket fence,

or merge into the background at a simple table. Use wood outdoors and feel yourself part of a great tradition.

credits

Architects and designers and useful addresses

Key: **a**=above, **b**=below, **l**=left, **r**=right, **t**=telephone, **f**=fax, **ph**=photographer

JoAnn Barwick, Interior Designer
P.O. Box 982
Boca Grande, FL 33921
Page 46 l

Ruby Beets
1703 Montauk Highway
Bridgehampton
New York, NY 11932
Page 15 r

Nancy Braithwaite Interiors
2300 Peachtree Road, Suite C101
Atlanta, GA 30309
Page 49

DAD Associates
112–116 Old Street
London EC1V 9BD
UK
t. 00 44 (0)20 7336 6488
Page 36

De Metz Architects
Unit 4
250 Finchley Road
London NW3 6DN
UK
t. 00 44 (0)20 7435 1144
Pages 4–5

Interni
Interior Design Consultancy
15–19 Boundary Street
Rushcutters Bay
Sydney, NSW 2011
Australia
Page 37 r

Jacomini Interior Design
1701 Brun, Suite 101
Houston, TX 77019
Page 31 r

Angela Kent (Architect)
Kenström Design Pty Ltd
92 Cathedral Street
Woolloomooloo, NSW 2011
Australia
Page 28 l

Holly Lueders Design
(Building, interior and
furniture design)
27 West 67 Street,
New York, NY 10023
Pages 15 r, 48, 55

Chris Ohrstrom
Historic Paints Ltd
Burr Tavern
Route 1, PO Box 474
East Meredith
New York, NY 13757
Page 35 br

Plain English Kitchen Design
The Tannery
Tannery Road
Coombs, Stowmarket
Suffolk IP14 2EN
UK
Pages 42–43

Mark Pynn A.I.A.
McMillen Pynn Architecture L.L.P.
P.O. Box 1068
Sun Valley, ID 83353
t. (208) 622 4656
f. (208) 726 7108
mpynn@sunvalley.net
www.sunvalleyarchitect.com
Page 26

Nico Rensch Architeam
UK
t 00 44 (0)411 412 898
Pages 37, 40

Jim Ruscitto (Architect)
Ruscitto, Latham, Blanton
PO Box 419
Sun Valley, ID 83353
Pages 2, 11, 14, 18–19

Allan Shope (Architect)
Shope, Reno, Wharton Associates
18 West Putnam Avenue
Greenwich, CT 06830
Page 20 r, 45 r

Stephen Varady Architecture
Studio 5
102 Albion Street
Surry Hills
Syndey, NSW 2010
Australia
Pages 23 l, 25

Olivier Vidal and Associates
(Architects)
14 rue Moncey
75009 Paris
France
Pages 29 r, 28–29

The Webb-Deane-Stevens Museum
211 Main Street
Wethersfield, CT 06109
Pages 34, 35 al

photographers

Front cover main ph James Merrell; **Front cover inset ph** Tom Leighton; **Back cover ph** James Merrell; **Spine ph** James Merrell; **Front flap ph** Simon Upton; **Back flap ph** James Merrell/Andrew Parr's house in Melbourne; **1 ph** James Merrell; **2 ph** James Merrell/a house in Idaho designed by Jim Ruscitto; **4–5 ph** Andrew Wood/Nicki De Metz's flat in London designed by De Metz Architects; **6 & 7 l & r ph** James Merrell; **8 ph** Andrew Wood; **9 ph** James Merrell; **11 ph** James Merrell/a house in Idaho designed by Jim Ruscitto; **12 l** Simon Upton; **12–13 & 13 ph** James Merrell; **14 ph** James Merrell/a house in Aspen designed by Jim Ruscitto; **15 l ph** James Merrell; **15 r ph** Fritz von der Schulenburg/Sharone Einhorn and Honey Walters' shop Ruby Beets in Bridgehampton; **16 ph** James Merrell/a lodge in Aspen designed by Holly Lueders Design; **17 ph** James Merrell; **18–19 ph** James Merrell/a house in Idaho designed by Jim Ruscitto; **20 l ph** James Merrell; **20 r ph** James Merrell/ a house in Connecticut designed by Allan Shope; **21 main and inset ph** James Merrell; **22 ph** James Merrell/Victor Ktori's loft in London designed by Circus Architects; **23 l ph** James Merrell/Linda Parham and David Slobham's apartment in Sydney designed by architect Stephen Varady; **23 r ph** Andrew Wood; **25 ph** James Merrell/Linda Parham and David Slobham's apartment in Sydney designed by architect Stephen Varady; **26 ph** James Merrell/chair designed by the architect Mark Pynn; **26-27 ph** Henry Bourne; **28 l ph** James Merrell/a house near Syndey designed by Angela Kent; **28–29 & 29 ph** James Merrell/a house in Paris designed by Olivier Vidal and Associates; **30 ph** James Merrell; **31 l ph** Catherine Gratwicke; **31 r ph** Simon Upton/a house in Texas designed by Jacomini Interior Design; **32 ph** James Merrell; **34 ph** James Merrell/The Webb-Deane-Stevens Museum; **35 al ph** James Merrell/The Webb-Deane-Stevens Museum; **35 ar ph** James Merrell; **35 bl ph** Henry Bourne; **35 br ph** James Merrell/Chris Ohrstrom Historic Paint Ltd; **36 ph** Henry Bourne/DAD Associates; **37 l ph** Andrew Wood/Andrew Noble's apartment in London designed By Nico Rensch Architeam; **37 r ph** James Merrell/Interni Interior Design Consultancy; **39 ph** Henry Bourne; **40–41 ph** Andrew Wood/Andrew Noble's apartment in London designed by Nico Rensch Architeam; **42–43 ph** Simon Upton/a kitchen designed by Plain English; **44 ph** James Merrell; **45 l ph** Tom Leighton/chairs by Twentieth Century Design; **45 r ph** James Merrell/a house in Connecticut designed by Allan Shope; **46 l ph** Simon Upton/a house designed by JoAnn Barwick; **46–47 ph** Tom Leighton/a loft in London designed by Robert Dye Associates; **48 ph** James Merrell/a lodge in Aspen designed by Holly Lueders Design; **49 ph** Simon Upton/a house designed by Nancy Braithwaite Interiors; **50 & 51 l ph** James Merrell; **51 r ph** Henry Bourne; **53 main ph** Andrew Wood; **53 inset ph** James Merrell; **54 al ph** Andrew Wood; **54 ar & bl ph** James Merrell; **54 br ph** Tom Leighton; **55 ph** James Merrell/a lodge in Aspen designed by Holly Lueders Design; **56 ph** James Merrell; **57 l ph** Tom Leighton; **57 r ph** Simon Upton; **58 ph** James Merrell; **59 ph** Simon Upton; **60 & 61 ph** Simon Upton; **61 r ph** James Merrell; **62–64 & Endpapers ph** James Merrell

The author and publisher would also like to thank all those whose homes or work are featured in this book.